ISABELLA

EVEN A STONE BREATHES

Even A Stone Breathes

Haiku & Senryu

Winona Baker

oolichan books

LANTZVILLE, BRITISH COLUMBIA, CANADA

2000

Canadian Cataloguing in Publication Data

Baker, Winona, 1924
        Even a stone breathes

Poems.
ISBN 0-88982-181-X

I. Title.

PS8553.A3855E93 2000   C811'.54   C00-910356-2

PR9199.3.B349E93 2000

We gratefully acknowledge the support of the Canada Council for the Arts for our publishing program.

THE CANADA COUNCIL | LE CONSEIL DES ARTS
FOR THE ARTS | DU CANADA
SINCE 1957 | DEPUIS 1957

Grateful acknowledgement is also made to the BC Ministry of Tourism, Small Business and Culture for their financial support.

We acknowledge the financial support of the Government of Canada through the Book Publishing Industry Development Program for our publishing activities.

Canadä

Published by
Oolichan Books
P.O. Box 10, Lantzville
British Columbia, Canada
V0R 2H0

Printed in Canada by
Morriss Printing Company
Victoria, British Columbia

for Art
and our family

Acknowledgements

Thanks to Myfanwy Spencer Pavelic and the Maltwood Gallery for permission to use the cover image "Rock Forms." The author would also like to express her gratitude to Ursula Vaira and Ron Smith for their fine editing, and to her writing group friends for listening and supporting. (Continued on page 73.)

Spring

old nun
sells ceramic babies
at the spring bazaar

spring cleaning—
dolls my daughter left
have slept twenty years

rocky hilltop
in a pocket of soil
green tips of shooting stars

last goodbye—
his ashes on the water
gold-flecked waves

for Brian

old pond—
frog's eggs float
in my reflection

such faint fragrance
in this unknown wildflower
I should not have picked

in the pocket
of his woodshed coveralls
a nest of deer mice

for Jim

grandson's plaque
on the memorial seawall
every wave different

feather
from an unknown bird
on the bracket fungus

the bear in the blossoms
holds out his arms
I do not understand

first narcissus—
rub soap in a collar
another age spot

warm gentle wind
cloudy— a perfect day
to wash an old quilt

wheelchair race—
white clover in the lawn
of the hospital

he mows the lawn in circles—
Basho's pond

washing windows
me inside   he outside
the smiling glass

dig new potatoes
'Look grandma—
a tired moon'

soft wind
carrying the scent of lilacs
through the screen door

freeway traffic
stalled both ways
skunk and kits crossing

another speech—
   wild flowers
on the CEO's table

sign QUIET
a pro tees off the green
a bird keeps singing

along the row
feeling guide wires
goes the blind gardener

feel sorry for the killer whale
she hasn't got a pod
to be in

prize sweet peas
where the outhouse was emptied
last spring

grandma's 'unders'
hang on the clothesline
inside pillow slips

Summer

beneath water
these stones
seem to be breathing

aviary—
birds watch children leaping
on the trampoline

tree trunk rounds
on the sawdusted lawn
under empty sky

sun bleaches
the spread linens
my son's hair

spider
hanging from the soffit
climbs into the cloud

young bald eagles—
unimpressive
without white crowns

summer radio
talks to empty rooms
faint sea sounds

low tide
    children walk from one island
        to the other

shore birds rise
  pulling the waves in
      fall   the waves retreat

beach
  waves arranging
    re-arranging

gull's awkward flight
with a fast food tray
over beach umbrellas

grandchild
snatched from the undertow
                    cries for her hat

        for Joan

moonlit beach
  I sit alone
on a driftwood log

stone beneath
my old sleeping bag—
falling star

lightning stab
   the cemetery poplar
riven

thunder storm—
the old Irish setter
trembles against me

waterfall
empties light
      into the river

river
   carries light
      to the sea

tree-filtered heat—
rivulets running down
the horse's flank

wild stallion
calls across the river—
the pack horse tenses

a field of melons—
remember Issa
'Turn into frogs'

in the flower bed
a man guts and fillets
a canary rock cod

cat's tail glides
through the long grass
faint bell sounds

shiver in sunlight—
outside the fortieth floor
a window cleaner

Autumn

hunter's moon—
waves lap the woman
carved in the rock

'Fourteen hundred feet . . . '
the open pit mine's depth—
we stand in sunlight

a dragonfly
on the lily pad
before that swallow

election speech—
purple loosestrife spreads
along the river

asked about smog
the politician said
'Just smells like money'

broad-leafed maple
turning golden from the top down—
colorless wind

autumn afternoon—
a kneeling gray-haired woman
clips grass on a grave

leaves soon to fall
the old one visits
a tree she planted

hike in falling leaves
the happiness
in the setter's tail

a spider spins
in the fisher's net
drying in the sun

barbershop fragrance
the autumn widow pauses
inhales

for Mae

blue heron flaps
over wind-buffeted trees—
lift grapes from the shadows

it's happened
my mother doesn't know me—
first autumn rain

slanted flying—*
a red leaf blows in
the open window

　　　　* *a movement in tai chi*

river mist
rises whitely behind a string
of wild horses

horse's muzzle
melts the moon
in the trough

crouched rabbit—
coat changing color
beside a peeling log

crows' whacking cries—
leaves fall from the poplar
in the cemetery

driving through mist
a white cat waits
by a mailbox

in the stubble
a ball of blue wool
unwinds in the wind

low tide
blue heron stalks
    the moving beach

parade over
vet stumbles down the street—
poppies in the gutter

heavy wind and rain—
the poplar
becoming anorexic

loon's wake
    and loon's cry
        becoming darkness

Winter

cold rain
the miner's gravestone
deeper in the earth

fourteen photos hang
over bouquets of flowers
propped in drifted snow

a gray sun
and a paper wasps' nest
in the bare tree

his size ten oxfords
on her dancing shoes—
even in the closet

floodlit yard—
cat's shadow on the aviary
a black panther

woman's solstice circle—
how warm the talking stone
passed to my hand

laughing Buddha
tinsel around his bald head
beneath the trimmed tree

smoke from a distant chimney—
first snowflakes disappear
in her white hair

poplar log
felled by beavers
burns in the fireplace

family visit:
he tries to fix what's wrong
with the answering machine

she and her doll
sleep after the party—
both one hundred today

Egypt disappoints—
she saw the pyramid
in Vegas

attic cobwebs—
a cracked window
and falling snow

coastline
wave and wind eroded
peeling arbutus

so cold
waiting for the school bus
children without hands

a dark path
in the graveyard
ends in a snowman

bare trees—
now there are mountains
on the mainland

(*with a bow to Basho*)

snowman
in the parking lot
anatomically correct

pale winter sunlight—
pine siskins at the feeder
wings flashing yellow

white-breath'd hooker
looks in the window
at the wedding gown

false teeth
frozen in the glass—
the cold

starched moon—
cold flannel arms
on the window sill

falling snow—
white envelopes drop
through the mail slot

the old dog
chained in the back yard
barks coldly

New Year

*In the old Japanese calendar New Year
was around the end of February. It was the
custom to write a haiku to celebrate the
coming of spring.*

Drawing

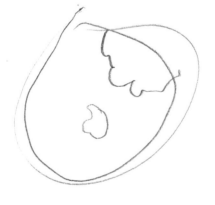

first dream—my old dog
paddles slowly with a stick
through the rosy waves

Index of First Lines

SPRING

SUMMER

AUTUMN

WINTER

NEW YEAR

ACKNOWLEDGEMENTS

The haiku and senryu in *Even a Stone Breathes* appeared in the following publications. The author would like to thank their editors.

NORTH AMERICA

JOURNALS

Brussels Sprout; Canadian Writers' Journal; Frogpond; Haiku Zasshi Zo; Honolulu Advertiser; Hwup!; Mirrors; Modern Haiku; Portal; RawNerVZ; Simcoe Review; Woodnotes.

CALENDARS

Burnished Pebbles, Timepieces 93, 94, 95, 96, 97

ANTHOLOGIES

An Invisible Accordion; Blue Spilling Over; Cold Morning; Dreams Wander; HEIWA: Peace Poetry in English and Japanese; Gathering Light; Light and Shadow; Northern Lights; One Breath; Palomar Showcase; Playing Tag Among The Buddhas; Scratch and Sniff; Solitary Leaf; Strong Winds; Through the Spirea; When Butterflies Come; Wild Strawberries.

EUROPE

England: Bare Bones; Blythe Spirit; The Haiku Calendar 2000; *Croatia*: Sparrow;. *Romania*: Albatross

ANTHOLOGY

The Art of Haiku 2000

JAPAN

PUBLICAATIONS

HI: Haiku International Journal, The Mainichi Daily
News; New Cicada

ANTHOLOGIES

Basho Festival Anthologies 95 & 96; HI Anthologies 92,
97; Haiku World- An International Poetry Almanac;
Iga-Ueno Basho Festival Anthology; Kasamakura
Anthology 98, 99; Mainichi Anthologies 97, 98.

DATE	ISSUED TO